Crickley Hill overlooks the Vale of Gloucester from the edge of the Costwold escarpment.
Right: the beautiful Norman church of St Peter and St Paul, Blockley.

- THE -
COTSWOLDS

Stephen Dorey

MYRIAD

Above and right: Cheltenham. During the Regency period Cheltenham Spa rivalled Bath in its splendour as the rich and the fashionable came to take the waters. Handel and Dr Johnson were among the town's notable visitors but the Spa reached the pinnacle of its success with the five-week visit of George III in 1788. The town retains an air of Georgian grandeur with spacious squares, crescents and formal gardens.

Above and right: Sudeley Castle. Set against the backdrop of the Cotswold hills, Sudeley Castle has over 14 acres of magnificent landscaped gardens. It was the home of Henry VIII's last wife, Catherine Parr, whose tomb is in St Mary's church next to the castle.

Above: the unspoilt town of Winchcombe is tucked away beneath the Cotswold edge, sheltered on three sides by pleasantly wooded hills. Winchcombe prospered thanks to the wool trade and its proximity to Sudeley Castle. Close by are the ruins of Hailes Abbey, a place of medieval pilgrimage.

Left: the "devil's chimney" in the quarry close to Leckhampton. The old village grew up around Leckhampton Court, one of the oldest manor houses in the county, and its church. The village retains much of its character despite now being a suburb of Cheltenham.

Right: the Mill Inn at Withington has the river Coln running through its garden and was once a water mill. To the south-east is the Roman villa of Chedworth. The villa was discovered by chance by a gamekeeper in 1864 and is one of the finest Roman villas in Britain.

Left: the village of Naunton lies in the upper Windrush valley and can often be seen in its entirety from nearby hills. The village has been a centre for sheep-rearing since it became monastic land in the Middle Ages.

Right: Guiting Power is situated on the river Windrush not far from Temple Guiting. The Temple part of its name comes from the 12th century when the manor was owned by the Knights Templar.

Left, right and below: Cirencester. An important city during the Roman era due to its location at the junction of three major roads: the Fosse Way, the Ermin Way and Akeman Street. The only visible remains of the Roman city in modern Cirencester are part of the old town wall and a turf-covered amphitheatre. The town's prosperity in the Middle Ages was aided by the presence of a large abbey and it eventually grew to pre-eminence in the wool trade. At the centre of Cirencester is its marketplace which is dominated by the 162ft (49m) high Perpendicular tower of its parish church – the largest in Gloucestershire.

Right and below: the small group of villages known as the Ampneys are found along the banks of the Ampney Brook. Down Ampney was the birthplace of the composer Ralph Vaughan Williams whose father was the vicar of All Saints (below). He composed the hymn tune *Down Ampney* (better known as *Come Down Oh Love Divine*) in honour of the village. Right: Ampney St Peter.

Above: Barnsley village is famous for Barnsley House with its attractive gardens designed in the 1950s by Rosemary Verey, one of Britain's most celebrated garden designers. She created a variety of garden types including an 18th-century herb garden, a knot garden, a laburnum walk and a vegetable garden. Barnsley House dates from 1697 when it was built for a local landowner, Brereton Bouchier.

Below: Northleach was one of the most important Cotswold wool towns in the Middle Ages. Its heyday as a medieval trading centre can still be seen in its magnificent church. This was largely rebuilt in the Perpendicular style in the 15th century and is a magnificent example of the style and period. The pinnacled south porch is said to be without equal in England and the tower combines both elegance and strength.

Left: while Bibury dates back to Saxon times, the bulk of the village owes its existence to the 17th-century wool trade. Arlington Row is a terrace of weavers' cottages that used to house workers from the nearby mill at Arlington. Rack Isle, in front of the cottages and now a nature reserve, was originally used for drying wool.

Above: the four villages that bear the name Duntisbourne are strung out in a line along the Dun Brook. From north to south they are: Duntisbourne Abbots, Duntisbourne Leer (above), Middle Duntisbourne and Duntisbourne Rouse.

Right: the ancient settlement of Snowshill is home to Snowshill Manor and its unusual museum established by Charles Paget Wade. Between 1900-1951 he built up a collection of 22,000 objects including automatons, butter stamps, bicycles, children's toys, clocks, cowbells, locks and 26 suits of Samurai armour.

Stow-on-the-Wold has the dubious distinction of being the highest town, at 800ft (244m), in the Cotswolds. A popular rhyme begins, "Stow-on-the-Wold, where the wind blows cold"; the shape of its unusual market square is in part dictated by the need for stallholders to be protected from the wind.

Above: Upper Slaughter. Although it sounds bloodthirsty, the name Slaughter is probably derived from the Old English word *slohtre* meaning slough or boggy place. The two villages that bear the name are both beautifully situated on the upper reaches of the river Eye. They are only about a mile away from each other, but they are very different in character.

Right: Lower Slaughter. The manor house in this beautiful village dates back to 1650 when it was built for Valentine Strong, the owner of a quarry at Little Barrington. The house has been remodelled since its construction but its grounds preserve one of the largest dovecotes in Gloucestershire. The Old Mill, with its large working water wheel and distinctive tall redbrick tower houses a cafe, museum and a small shop.

Left, right and above: Moreton-in-Marsh. Straddling the Fosse Way, the location of Moreton-in-Marsh accounts for its existence and prosperity. During the 17th and 18th centuries it was on the main coaching route between London, Oxford, Worcester and Hereford. When coaching declined the town quickly moved on to railways; the Stratford-Moreton tramway opened in 1826 and was one of the earliest railways in the country. As a centre for travellers Moreton-in-Marsh is well provided with inns one of which, the 16th-century White Hart (Royal) Hotel, was used by Charles I during the Civil War.

Left: Blockley. This was one of the first villages in England to produce its own electricity, thanks to the power of the Blockley Brook. In previous centuries the brook provided the energy for corn mills, silk throwers and even wood saws. Six mills once operated in the village.

Right: Saintbury. Ranged along the side of Saintbury Hill the village has a fine cross which stands at the crossroads to the north of the village. The lower part dates from the 15th century whilst the Maltese cross and sundial were added in 1848.

Left, right and below: Chipping Campden. Its name is derived from the word "chipping", an Old English word meaning market; it was as a wool and cattle market that the village first grew up. The market hall was built in 1627. St James' church is a significant local landmark and features a 15th-century pinnacled tower. It houses some interesting marble monuments, brasses and an excellent collection of English medieval embroidery.

Left, right and above: Broadway. This stunning village is regarded by many as the finest large village in the Cotswolds. As its name suggests, it has a wide main street and it was once an important staging post on the London to Worcester route. A new turnpike was opened in 1736 and at one time seven coaches passed through the village each day. Many of the fine buildings along Broadway's main street began their lives as inns to serve the passing trade. With the coming of the railways the coach trade declined but Broadway had its own station and it quickly became a stopping off point for exploration of the Cotswolds.

Essentially a single street village, Stanton is claimed by many to be one of the oldest in the Cotswolds. Most of its houses date from the 17th century. The village was extensively restored by the architect Sir Philip Stott after he purchased large tracts of it just before the First World War.

Right: the large hamlet of Laverton is located beneath the Cotswold edge. It contains several substantial and well-built farmhouses that date back to the 16th century and make good use of local stone. Laverton is close to the Cotswold Way and the many fine views in the area make it popular with walkers. Broadway to the north and Stanton to the south are both within easy reach.

Left: Burford, the eastern gateway to the Cotswolds. The town built its reputation on wool, quarrying and coaching. Wool was important from the 14th century onwards and the stone from nearby quarries was used in the construction of some of Britain's finest buildings, ranging from Blenheim Palace to St Paul's Cathedral. Burford's heyday as a coaching town came in the 18th century when it was an important stop on routes into Oxford and London.

Left and above: Stanway. The village is dominated by the gatehouse to Stanway House. Built during the 1580s on the site of an earlier manor house it is mostly Jacobean in style and has a remarkable 60-pane oriel window. The grounds contain a water garden which features the highest fountain in England, a tithe barn dating from 1370 and a log-fired brewing house.

Below and right: five ornamental bridges span the river Windrush in Bourton-on-the-Water giving the village the nickname of the "Venice of the Cotswolds". Bourton-on-the-Water is served by the parish church of St Lawrence. In 1784 the Norman church was largely replaced with today's neo-Classical style building with its thick tower housing a clock and bells. Further additions were made in the 1870s when the present nave was constructed. The nave roof is a fine example of a king-post roof.
Left: Bourton-on-the-Hill.

Right: Miserden. This village has had a long history of growth, decay and renewal. The church has late Saxon origins although it was extensively restored in the 1880s. The war memorial was designed by Sir Edwin Lutyens.

Above and right: Stroud. Five valleys meet here making it a natural centre for trade and transport. In the Middle Ages Stroud established itself as a centre of the cloth industry; at the height of its prosperity there were 150 mills in and around the town. Stroud was particularly famous for making the cloth used in military uniforms. The centre of Stroud reflects its role as a market town with its many narrow streets, its Tudor town hall and the Shambles, the area for butchers.

Left, right and below: Castle Combe. Although it is well to the south of the area, Castle Combe displays many of the charms of a traditional Cotswold village. It is centred on a market cross that reflects its growth through wool trading. Other marks of this industry include several fine timber-framed buildings and the substantial Perpendicular tower that was added to the church in 1434. The village is situated on the By Brook and a charming bridge spans the stream here.

Left and right: to the south-west of the area, and largely built of Cotswold stone, Bath has had two major heydays. The first was during the Roman occupation when the town of *Aqua Sulis* grew up around its natural hot springs and the second was during the Regency and Georgian periods when the craze for taking the waters made Bath one of the largest cities in England. Substantial traces of both periods can still be seen in the city. Apart from the Roman baths and the temple, the ancient city largely disappeared during the Saxon period and it was largely in royal and monastic hands throughout the Middle Ages. The spa trade revived after the Dissolution of the Monasteries but it was not until after the Civil War that Bath began to be a health centre for the aristocracy. The new Bath was largely built in the Classical style with long stretches of identical façades to give an impression of palatial scale and Classical decorum.